THE GRUMMAN XF10F-1

BY C. H. "CORKY" MEYER FORMER GRUMMAN TEST PILOT AND ONLY PILOT EVER TO FLY THE X...

INTRODUCTION

Since the early days of flight when the takeoff speed was just under the top speed of an airplane, designers have sought many different ways to make the ratio of the takeoff speed to the top speed greater and greater.

Increase in power was the simplest answer, but then the aircraft weight went up, and the takeoff speed increased, and the flying fields got too small. Putting a bigger wing on the airplane got the takeoff distance back to the airfield size, but the speed then suffered. It seemed clearly obvious that if one could have a wing that was big enough to use the small size of the flying fields for takeoff and then shrink it when in the air, one could have the best of all worlds: good takeoff performance coupled with much better high-speed performance.

The present day high-lift knowledge by the use of highly complicated flaps, slats, boundary layer control, fences, vortex generators etc., took a long time in coming and a lot of research and development by sophisticated means of wind tunnels that were not available or timely for the designers prior to World War Two. Although there were many pioneering variable geometry aircraft that actually were built, only a few of them were remarkable.

In 1931, the French expatriate Russian designer Ivan Makhonine de-vised the MAK-10, which was a low-wing monoplane which extended its wing span by shrinking into itself from 68 feet to 42 feet, thereby decreasing its area almost 33 percent. The data showed that some performance gains were made, but the complexities of the design were enormous, and the idea was not tested to the extent that it might have been were it designed by one of the larger French companies at

---

Head-on view of the mock-up of the Grumman XF10F Jaguar. Because of the aircraft's swing-wing design the main gear had to be fitted into the fuselage sides as seen here. A very similar nose gear would be used on the F11F Tiger. (Grumman)

The Bell X-5 which was tested at the same time as the XF10F-1 Jaguar.

the time who could have put the proper monies and thus effort into good designs.

A MAK-101 was being developed after World War Two started, but the designer, in a fit of patriotism, had the test pilot crash it to prevent it from falling into German hands. After the war, the MAK-123 was flown, but although the wing extension worked as advertised, the airplane had a forced landing in a potato field early in its test program and was never flown again.

The Russians had an entirely different solution to this problem: their RK-1 piston engine powered biplane fighter in 1938 that retracted the wheels into the lower wing then promptly retracted the lower wing up into an indentation in the lower surface of the upper wing. This reduced the wing area by 40 percent and gave this biplane a speed of 281 mph in 1939. There is little more known of its per-

Below, the Grumman/Navy F-111B.

formance, but this was the first variable geometry fighter designed from start as a production airplane. Although the results were pronounced "promising," no more was seen of this airplane.

The Messerschmitt people started a design in June 1944 of a mid-wing jet fighter known as the P-1101 which was to have a wing that could be positioned only on the ground to sweep from 0 to 40 degrees and then flight test any angles in between. This airplane was not finished, but it was brought over to the United States immediately after the war when we were "requisitioning" German talents like the Russians were.

Once in the United States the aircraft was given to Bell to redesign the airplane so that it would be able to move the wings in flight by the use of electric motors with a wing carriage that moved back and forth in the fuselage about 39 inches during the process. The mechanism was heavy and cumbersome. The Bell X-5 was flown many times at Edwards AFB, California, and a great deal of data was obtained from these flights. I was

supposed to evaluate it, but the flight before I was to fly it, the test pilot got into a spin, could not recover, and was killed. No more prototypes were made. The X-5 was flying when we were flying the Grumman XF10F-1 Jaguar at Edwards in 1952. The XF10F-1 was the first aircraft to be designed from the ground up as a production variable geometry airplane.

Although the XF10F-1 never entered production, the experience gained with its variable geometry wing stood the Navy in good stead over the years. As I was the only one who ever sat in the XF10F-1 when the engine was running, you can well imagine that when the great F-111 multi-service airplane was remanded to the McClelland Committee in the Senate investigation to determine why the contract was given to General Dynamics instead of Boeing, my services were in demand by General Dynamics, Grumman being the subcontractor for the naval version. We were pleased to be able to respond to Boeing's allegation that they had "thousands of hours of wind tunnel time with variable geometry airplanes" by saying that we had that too, plus we had one year's testing of a real variable geometry airplane....in the air, and we would like to have the test pilot who flew it tell you all about it! It may have been coincidental, but after my pitch, the McClelland Committee investigation ended on that very day.

Getting the F-111B subcontract of the naval version was not a real win in the production experience sense, but during the hundreds of flights on these five Navy airplanes, Grumman again got much air-practical experience on variable geometry aircraft to make our proposal a winning one when the F-14 program came along several years later. The Navy was able to benefit from the XF10F-1 and the F-111B experience in the past, present, and future years of Tomcat dominance in the fighter skies. It surely does help to have flown the birds when it comes time to have the capability to win a contract or a war. As Orville Wright stated so succinctly, "the only way to really know how to fly a machine is to mount it, take it up into the air, and actually find out how it behaves." Together, Grumman and the Navy did just that to get the best fighter in the skies for years to come: the F-14 Tomcat.

DEVELOPMENT

On 3 September 1947, Grumman submitted its design 83 proposal for a swept-wing jet fighter. On 16 December 1947, the Bureau of Aeronautics issued a letter of intent covering the development of the XF9F-2 Panther which also requested an engineering proposal of a swept-wing version. The original design 83 looked very much like an RF-84 or a Gnat fighter with a "T" tail. The design was so radically different than the XF9F-2 that it was designated XF10F-1 on 4 March 1948. On 7 April a letter of intent was issued to Grumman for two XF10F-1s. In November the design had changed into a ship that resembled the final test article. The wing was of the variable-incidence type and the horizontal tail was mounted on the fuselage sides. Also in 1948 Grumman submitted design 86, which was an XF10F-1 with redesigned intakes and wings that was fitted with a 5,000 pound thrust rocket motor mounted beneath the fuselage.

The XF10F-1 drawings were converted to hardware in April 1949 when the mock-up was reviewed by the Navy. With the inspection came changes in requirements and configurations which added more weight to the original design. It was at this point, 7 July 1949, that Grumman formally proposed a variable-swept-wing fighter to make carrier operations feasible. Along with the change to a variable-swept-wing came a revision to the horizontal tail which meant a return to the "T" tail configuration. The Navy was given a letter of intent on 18 August 1950 for 12 XF10F-1s. This was followed by a formal contract on 14 December and a subsequent order for a further 70 Jaguars on 10 February 1951. The first and only flyable XF10F-1 was completed in early 1952, and after low-speed taxi runs at Bethpage it was flown aboard a C-124 to Edwards on 16 April 1952.

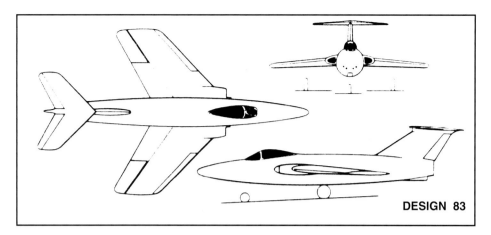

DESIGN 83

Design 83 would have had a span of 32 feet 4 inches, a length of 49 feet 6 inches and be powered by a Pratt & Whitney J42 jet engine rated at 5,000 pounds thrust. Empty weight was to have been 10,121 pounds and takeoff weight was 18,729 pounds. Stall speed on takeoff was estimated at 100 knots, landing stall speed was to be 85 knots. High speed level flight was to be 596 knots with a rate of climb of 11,650 feet per minute. Endurance was estimated at 4.05 hours at a radius of 468 nautical miles. Armament was to be four 20-mm cannons in the nose.

Design 83 (second version, XF10F) maintained the same length as the original design 83. Wing span would have been 29 feet 7 inches, and the engine was changed to the Pratt & Whitney J48 of 6,500 pounds thrust. Empty weight was 11,402 pounds and takeoff weight was 20,000 pounds. High speed level flight increased to 635 knots with a rate of climb of 14,750 feet per minute. Endurance suffered greatly by this design and dropped to 2.96 hours or a radius of 295 nautical miles. The cannon armament remained the same.

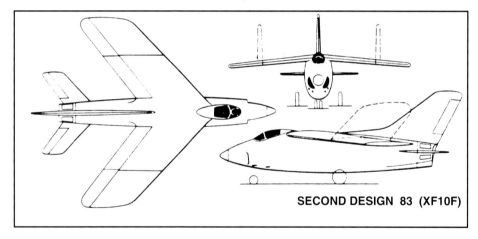

SECOND DESIGN 83 (XF10F)

Below, Design 86 was proposed as a pure interceptor version of the Design 83 (XF10F) with a 5,000 pound Curtiss-Wright rocket motor beneath the fuselage.

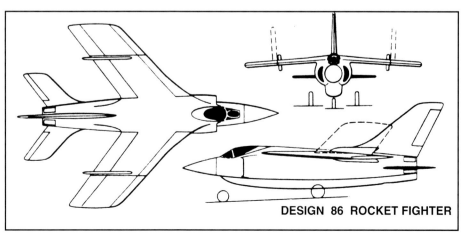

DESIGN 86 ROCKET FIGHTER

At left, flying model of XF10F that showed the design to have poor longitudinal characteristics. Engineers did not believe in these results nor wind tunnel tests, however their predictions came true in the completed aircraft. The model was built by Joseph Lippert.

Above, the original XF10F-1 mock-up in April 1947 (second design 83). This design had a conventional tail with a fixed ventral fin and a sweptback variable incidence wing. The vertical tail was cut off to clear the overhead. (Grumman)

Bottom, the final XF10F-1 design in final construction on 3-7-52. Final configuration differed from the mock-up in having a swing-wing and a double delta "T" tail. (Grumman)

G-43067

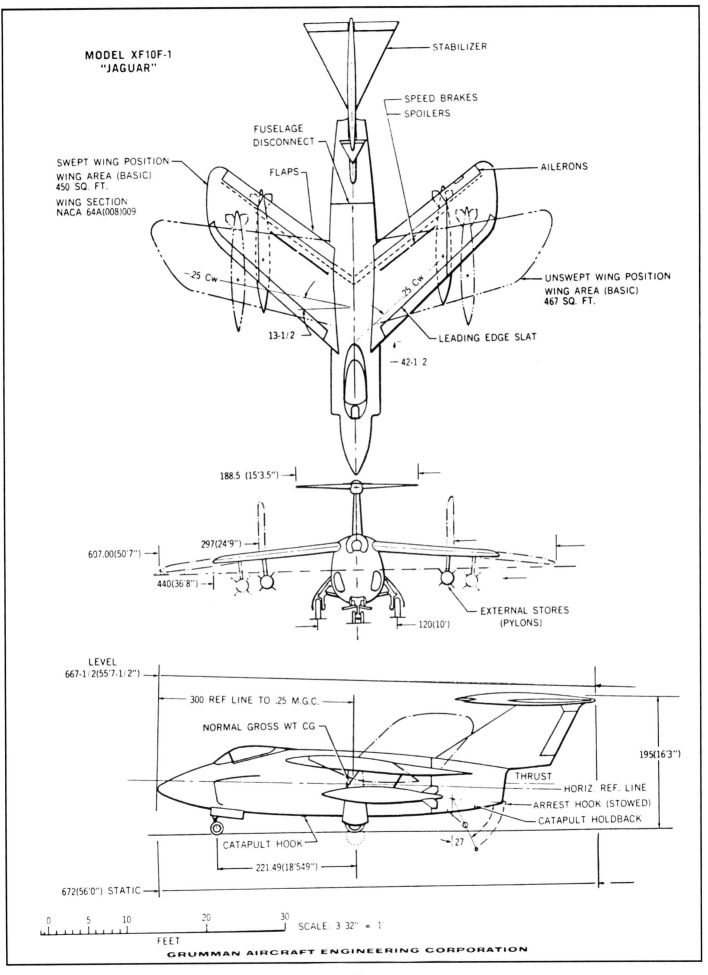

MODEL XF10F-1
"JAGUAR"

STABILIZER

SPEED BRAKES
SPOILERS

FUSELAGE
DISCONNECT

FLAPS

AILERONS

SWEPT WING POSITION
WING AREA (BASIC)
450 SQ. FT.

WING SECTION
NACA 64A(008)009

.25 Cw

.25 Cw

UNSWEPT WING POSITION
WING AREA (BASIC)
467 SQ. FT.

13-1/2

LEADING EDGE SLAT

42-1/2

188.5 (15'3.5")

607.00(50'7")

297(24'9")

440(36'8")

EXTERNAL STORES
(PYLONS)

120(10')

LEVEL
667-1/2(55'7-1/2")

300 REF LINE TO .25 M.G.C.

NORMAL GROSS WT CG

195(16'3")

THRUST

HORIZ. REF. LINE

ARREST HOOK (STOWED)

CATAPULT HOLDBACK

27

CATAPULT HOOK

221.49(18'549")

672(56'0") STATIC

0   5   10   20   30   SCALE: 3 32" = 1'

FEET

GRUMMAN AIRCRAFT ENGINEERING CORPORATION

6

DESCRIPTION OF THE FLIGHT TEST XF10F-1 AIRCRAFT

The XF10F-1 was designed as a single seat, long-range, general purpose, carrier or land based, transonic fighter whose primary mission was to intercept and destroy enemy aircraft. It was designed to operate from CV-34 or CVB class aircraft carriers.

WEIGHTS

EMPTY	20,468
TAKEOFF	31,255
MAX TAKEOFF	35,370
(2-300 GAL. WING TANKS)	
MAX LANDING	27,700

DIMENSIONS

WING AREA (STRAIGHT WING)	467 SQ. FT.
WING AREA (SWEPT WING)	450 SQ. FT.
SPAN (STRAIGHT WING)	50 FT. 7 IN.
SPAN (SWEPT WING)	36 FT. 8 IN.
SPAN (SWEPT/FOLDED)	24 FT. 9 IN.
SPAN TAILPLANE (DOUBLE DELTA)	15 FT. 3.5 IN.
LENGTH	55 FT. 7 IN.
HEIGHT	16 FT. 3 IN.
TREAD	10 FT.

FUEL AND OIL

WING TANKS (2)	548 GALS.
FUSELAGE (3)	1,037 GALS.
DROP TANKS (2)	600 GALS.
FUEL GRADE	JP-3
FUEL SPEC.	MIL-F-5624
OIL	41 GALS.
GRADE	1010
SPEC.	MIL-0-6081

ELECTRONICS

ADF	AN/ARN-6
ALTIMETER	AN/APN-1,-22
HOMING	AN/ARN-2A
IFF	AN/APX-6
SEARCH RADAR	AN/APQ-41
UDF D. F.	AN/ARA-25
VHF	AN/ARC-27
PLANNED SERVICE INSTALLATION	
IFF (IR UNIT)	AN/APX-17
1 CHANNEL UHF	AN/ARC-
VOR	AN/ARN-21
(TO REPLACE AN/ARN-6)	

POWER PLANT

MODEL	J-40-WE-8
MFR	WESTINGHOUSE
AB	INTEGRAL
TYPE	14 STAGE AXIAL
LENGTH	287 IN.
DIAMETER	43 IN.
THRUST (NORMAL)	6,700 LBS.
THRUST (MILITARY)	7,400 LBS.
THRUST (MILITARY WITH AFTERBURNER)	10,900 LBS.

During the flight test period of the Jaguar, however, the afterburner had not been developed so only 7,200 pounds of thrust could be obtained. Without the afterburner, the unfavorable thrust-to-weight ratio caused a severe limitation on test altitudes.

ORDNANCE

GUNS	4-20 MM.
ROCKETS FFAR	2X24 PODS
BOMBS	2X2,000 LBS.
INTERCEPT ARMAMENT CONTROL SYSTEM	AERO-6B

To provide for external store and fuel capabilities, bomb racks were installed on the wing with swivel-type pylons which kept the racks aligned with the centerline of the airplane as the wing sweep angle was changed.

WING-SWEEP MECHANISM

The wing sweep angle could be varied in flight from 13.5 to 42.5 degrees and the wing sweep mechanism was designed to be operable through-out the entire 7g structural flight envelope of the airplane. When swept back from the straight position, the wing translated forward along the fuselage and simultaneously rotated inward. The wing motion was provided by one hydraulic cylinder. The enlightened days of dual powered aircraft systems had not yet arrived. Wind tunnel tests had indicated that the wing would sweep naturally into the straight position by aerodynamic forces if the hydraulic system failed. Fortunately, during the test program the hydraulic system almost functioned without failure.

To utilize the variable sweep thoroughly in the straight wing takeoff and landing configurations, the airplane had full span aerodynamic slats and 80% span Fowler-type landing flaps. The flaps were unusable in the swept position because the inboard end projected into the fuselage.

The wing center of pressure travel had very little longitudinal motion during wing sweep. As a matter of fact, on the last two flights of the airplane, when a power-boosted, high-aspect ratio tail was installed, less

Swing-wing pivot forging for the XF10F-1 as seen on 29 June 1951. (Grumman via Nicolaou)

than 1/2 degree of stabilizer motion was necessary to counteract the effect of wing sweep motion under any flight condition. With the low aspect ratio double-delta tail on the airplane, however, the change in trim with flap extension and retraction was extremely high.

LATERAL CONTROL

Lateral control of the airplane was provided by a series of eight paddle spoilers which extended through a slot in the wing immediately forward of the flaps. These spoilers had 180 degrees of motion so they would have an effect both above and below the wing similar to ailerons.

Since the paddle spoilers came out normal to the chord plane, it was assumed that they would have little or no associated stick forces, so small aerodynamically balanced ailerons were incorporated on the wing to provide feel to the pilot. It was soon learned, however, that these spoilers not only had large, but very erratic, forces, and produced flutter on almost every flight that they were used. A power boost system was added to this control later in the program, but it was unwisely incorporated near the cockpit, which had the effect of only delaying flutter to much higher air speed. This system was finally rendered inoperative.

In addition, the wing slot itself had a detrimental effect on the static and dynamic lateral-directional characteristics. Consequently, most of the flights were carried out using only the small ailerons for all of the lateral control. The spoilers and slot were finally eliminated and covered over.

The lateral-directional flight characteristics of the XF10F were probably its most significant problem area. As soon as it was determined that the spoiler-type lateral control itself and the continuous slot through the wing were producing built-in difficulties, the spoiler mechanism and the slots were eliminated, with a resultant large improvement in the lateral-directional flight characteristics.

In the straight wing configuration

the airplane had ideal static and dynamic lateral-directional flight characteristics. Roll due to yaw was very low through neutral in the clean configuration, and the wing could be readily raised with rudder in the landing configuration. The airplane exhibited very good directional damping and, in general, had flight characteristics similar to the straight wing jet fighters of the day.

However, when the wings were swept, the dihedral effect changed considerably, and the project aerodynamicist stated that it would be impossible to supply sufficient negative dihedral to balance this change by geometric means. In the swept-

Above, paddle spoilers as seen deployed on the upper wing. (Grumman via Nicolaou)

wing condition the airplane showed a marked decrease in directional stability which further aggravated these parameters so that acceptable test data could be taken only in relatively smooth air.

Based on the state-of-the-art of yaw dampers at the time, it was clear that a very powerful yaw damper and a large increase in directional stability would be necessary to correct these

Below, paddle spoilers from below. (Grumman via Nicolaou)

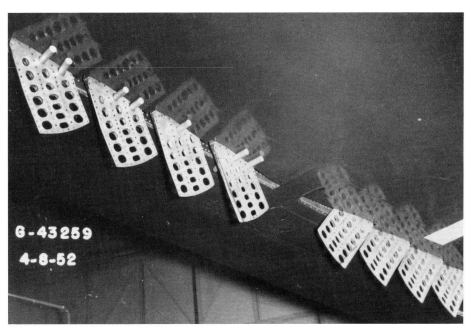

lateral-directional characteristics.

HORSAL FINS

To increase the directional stability, horsal fins were added to the airplane with surprising effects. (The word "horsal" resulted from the American penchant for combining words ---- horizontal-dorsals.)

Not only was the directional stability increased by this addition, but the roll due to yaw was reduced by a sufficient factor so that the flight characteristics were then acceptable. Bear in mind that at this time, however, the lateral and directional controls consisted only of the small aerodynamic ailerons and a rudder that was undersized for the airplane. With these small controls, it was impossible to deflect the airplane flight path to any great degree. Had there been effective lateral and directional controls, other problems in this area might have been uncovered.

It is interesting to note that the National Advisory Committee for Aeronautics had configured a Grumman Hellcat to allow lateral and directional stability parameters to be varied in flight. Prior to flying the XF10F, I flew this airplane with the XF10F parameters inserted into the stability control boxes. The lateral-directional flight characteristics in the

View of horsal fins that were tested to increase directional stability. (Grumman)

simulated swept wing condition were so bad that neither I nor anyone else connected with the XF10F program believed them. However, we were to learn later that the predictions of the NACA group were correct. After I flew the XF10F-1, we then realized that such characteristics could be predicted very accurately prior to flight, by people who were not proud parents of the design.

LONGITUDINAL FLIGHT CHARACTERISTICS

The double-delta tail which was installed on the airplane for all but the last three flights was so influenced by the stall flow that it was impossible to maneuver the airplane for the last 30 knots preceding the stall. Consequently, the stall characteristics could not be properly investigated until the last two flights when the power-boosted, higher aspect ratio horizontal tail was installed.

Using the powered tail, it was found that the stall characteristics were quite good until pitch-up occurred within a few knots of the stall, followed by strong roll-off. A logical cure for this pitch-up and / or roll-off during that time period would have

been fences. However, it would have been impossible to put a fence on this airplane with a variable sweep wing.

The addition of the horsals reduced pre-stall pitch-up considerably and gave the airplane satisfactory landing stall characteristics. However, the horsal fin area was probably too small to have any significant effect on the clean condition swept wing pitch-up. Unfortunately, other aspects of the flight test program precluded delving into this interesting area of the flight envelope. In addition, the horsals proved to be a serious problem to ground maintenance personnel ----- they were sharply pointed and located in a position on the airplane such that someone inevitably walked into them almost every day.

The longitudinal maneuvering flight characteristics were also affected to a large degree by changing the wing sweep angle. Again, the longitudinal maneuvering qualities appeared to be optimized for the straight wing airplane. As soon as the wing was swept, the maneuvering forces increased by a factor of about 3. Had the airplane gone into production with an aerodynamic control on it (which was the original premise), great difficulty would have been encountered in getting a proper balance of maneuvering forces between these two sweep angles. This will still be somewhat of a problem today with power operated controls and stability augmentation.

CONTROL SURFACE SIZING

The variable wing geometry of the XF10F also brought out other effects of the vast speed range possible for an airplane of its size and inertia. The rudder control was over-sized for high speed flight characteristics, but was only about 1/4 the size necessary at speeds close to the straight wing stall. Even the high aspect ratio powered longitudinal control surface presented the same deficiency, as did the lateral control, though to a lesser degree. A fully powered longitudinal control might have solved the problem on the XF10F, but it is believed that if the airplane had gone into production, a high aspect ratio tail of even twice the size of the one installed for the last two flights would have been required.

SPEED REDUCTION

Speed brakes were deliberately omitted in the original XF10F design, since it was thought that the variable sweep wing would serve the same function. Although the wing did provide exceptionally good speed reduction as the sweep angle was decreased, the airplane, in the straight wing configuration, also required speed brakes. Because of the unique design of the XF10F, it became a major task to locate adequate sized speed brakes on the airplane after it had been built and flown.

VARIABLE GEOMETRY PERFORMANCE EFFECTS

To visualize more fully the effects of the variable sweep wing on the XF10F, it is of interest to compare it with another Navy airplane, the McDonnell F3H, which was developed in the same time period and which had very similar geometric proportions.

The size, weight, wing area, and wing sweep angle are approximately the same as the XF10F. Because of this geometric similarity and the fact that both airplanes utilized the J40 engine, maximum level flight speeds were nearly the same. In the landing configuration, however, the stall speed of the Jaguar was 78 knots, as compared to 96 knots for the F3H, or a difference of 18 knots, thereby giving the XF10F-1 over a 20 knot improvement in approach speeds.

Practical experience showed further that a straight wing carrier jet airplane could be flown at an approach speed much closer to the stall than a swept wing airplane due to its lower attitude angle, better lift distribution characteristics, etc. Therefore, the XF10F had an even greater safety margin in approach. Cruise flight performance of the XF10F also demonstrated validity and worth of the variable wing geometry.

The weight penalty of the variable sweep feature in the XF10F-1 was

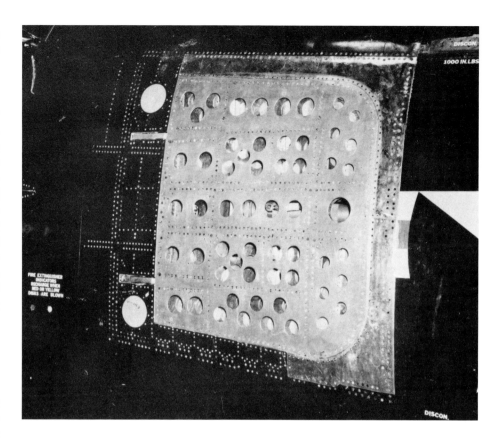

calculated to be approximately 1,500 pounds of additional structure. The difference in stall speed between the XF10F and F3H airplanes, however, shows that the XF10F had a margin of approximately 12,000 pounds in growth potential, thereby proving that the weight penalty was small in comparison to the benefits provided by the wing.

The fuselage speed brakes were added on the 17th. flight. Above, speed brakes in the closed position. (Grumman) Below, speed brakes in the open position. (Grumman via Nicolaou)

FLYING THE GRUMMAN XF10F-1 JAGUAR

The Grumman XF10F Jaguar was designed with a variable-sweep wing for one reason alone: to render a heavy swept-wing combat aircraft compatible with the aircraft carrier from which it was intended to operate. The high takeoff and landing speeds of such aircraft were understandably arousing intense concern in US Navy circles in the early fifties. There was some justification for believing that a fighter fitted with a highly-loaded swept wing would never be able to get down to approach and stalling speeds acceptable for shipboard operation, and since accident attrition varied with the rate of speed increase squared, there was the possibility of an impasse in shipboard fighter development. It was thus as a possible solution to the problem of safely launching and retrieving the up-and-coming generation of swept-wing combat aeroplanes in carrier operations that Grumman adopted the highly innovative approach of varying wing sweep.

Insofar as the achievement of this primary aim was concerned, the XF10F program may be considered to have been a resounding success. We eventually brought the stalling speed

down to 78 knots. This represented a fantastic lift coefficient for an airplane weighing 31,500 pounds with a mere 6,800 pounds of installed thrust ---- a poorer thrust-to-weight ratio than that of a Boeing 747!

I was to be the only pilot ever to fly the sole example of the XF10F-1 completed. We had incorporated so many novel ideas into the airplane and suffered so many teething troubles with these and with the engine that we never seemed to find enough time to check out another pilot! On the first taxi runs made at Bethpage, I accelerated the aircraft up to 80-90 mph and pulled back on the stick. The nosewheel lifted off and the tail bumper wheel hit the ground ---and stayed there. I pushed the stick forward but the big canard tail stayed down as there was not enough servo plane power to raise it. I did not need much convincing that I had a control surface over which I had anything but control. The only way to raise the tail was to hit the brakes and bring the nosewheel back on the ground. This confirmed the high inertia and low control power of the horizontal tail previously encountered in wind tunnel

The XF10F-1 at roll-out on 4-12-52 at Grumman Bethpage. (Grumman via Nicolaou)

and control line model tests, but because the project engineer, Gordon Israel, had implicit faith in the tail, we proceeded with flight testing at Edwards AFB.

At Edwards I made many taxi runs to lift-off speed and actually raised the XF10F-1 into the air for 10 to 12 seconds before putting it back on the ground. Many of these so-called "taxi" runs were, in fact, flights though unrecognised as such by the Navy as none included a complete circuit of the field. In consequence, although the XF10F-1 was to go on record as having made only 32 flights, the number of lift-offs actually made exceeded 200!

As the taxi runs built up I became increasingly frustrated but I was still reluctant to commit myself to a genuine attempt to fly the airplane. On one occasion I lifted off for about 20 seconds and as I put the XF10F-1 down, Bob Mullaney, our propulsion expert,

heard over the radio a loud "Oh ------!" Knowing that I had flown too far down the runway and fearing the worst, he leaped into the crash truck and found me sitting about a hundred yards out into the sand, beyond the end of the runway. That episode made up my mind for me --- I would not commit myself to a real attempt to fly the aircraft until we could get it down onto the lake bed and I could lift off for a minute or so of straight-ahead flight and really feel out the XF10F-1.

Eventually, on 19 May 1952, I managed to get the XF10F-1 up to between 150 and 160 knots at which the balanced tail was more effective, and so I took-off at 0752 hours and, once in the air, found that I was unable to retract the wing slats so I could not get above 200 knots. I climbed to

XF10F-1 on 4-12-52 with slats down and four of the paddle spoilers visible beneath the wing. (Grumman)

Close-up shows steps, handholds and stenciling details. Test instruments are loaded in the cannon bay. (Grumman)

about 8,000 feet to do some stalls, but when I tried to retract the flaps I discovered that the change in trim with flap movement used up all stick motion --- if I selected "flaps up" I had to apply full forward stick and anything more than half-flap demanded full aft stick. I then throttled back the engine and the airplane oscillated violently and yawed about 20 degrees. It was subsequently ascertained that this

was because the clamshell nozzle caused the jet exhaust to impinge on the bottom of the fin-and-rudder assembly when the two vertical halves closed to constrict the flow, and a horizontal fence was fitted to the bottom of the vertical fin for the second flight. There was very little I could do apart from making a rather careful circuit of the field and land, only 16 minutes having elapsed from takeoff.

The XF10F-1 being serviced at Bethpage on 4-12-52. (via Nicolaou)

The second flight was attempted two days later, and at between 10,000 and 12,000 feet above the lake bed on a very calm morning I was just about

Close-up of the original double-delta "T" tail as seen on 4-12-52. Note small size of the rudder. (Grumman)

to stall the airplane for the first time when it was rocked by a very violent explosion and pitched up! I hurriedly shut down the engine and began a gliding descent. The accompanying chase plane pulled out ahead of me as my speed was so low and as I came in to a deadstick landing I suddenly realized that the pilot of the chase plane had forgotten to lower his wheels. I yelled at him over the radio as he hit on flaps and tailplane, fortunately bouncing high enough to lower his wheels for a normal rollout, but my landing, meanwhile, had to be seen to be believed, the XF10F-1 leaping all over the place, practically out of control. The best thing that anyone could say about that landing was that it was short!

Once on the ground, we gingerly ran up the engine and checked everything, but we could find nothing that could account for that explosion. We decided, therefore, to risk a further flight the next day, and the unnerving phenomenon did not repeat itself, at least, on that occasion. Several flights later, two more violent explosions took place in the engine bay. This time I was completely spooked. No warning had preceded the explosions; I was not changing attitude, moving the throttle, or anything at all other than flying sedately along, straight and level. Such had been the violence of the explosions that Bob Mullaney had heard both of them on the ground, but Bob, bless his heart, would not have worried had the devil been telling him

"Corky" Meyers conducting taxi tests at Bethpage. The small protrusion in front of the windscreen was a barricade deflector which extended whenever the canopy was open. (Grumman)

what to do, and concluded that the electronic fuel control was the culprit. The engine manufacturer, Westinghouse, told us that we should not open up the control unit which should be returned to the factory, complete with Navy seal, but Bob said that we would open it up and we did.

Head-on view showing contrast between the delta tail and the wings when they were swept forward. (Grumman)

The unit was some 24 inches in length and 7 inches wide, and we removed all the screws around the edges of the unit and attempted to pry open the top. This refused to budge. Something was holding down the manufacturers identification plate. We removed one of these screws and it proved to be of the length that we had anticipated, merely holding the plate in position, but the second screw kept coming, proving to be one-and-a-quarter inches in length and going right down into the guts of the fuel control. Some damned careless character had taken this oversized screw and pushed it straight into the bundles of wire, crystals and what have you! We installed another fuel control and at least that problem never repeated itself.

During its test program the XF10F-1 was never to be flown above 25,000 feet except on its twentieth flight on 11 October 1952, when I took it up to 31,500 feet, the unreheated service ceiling of the airplane, for high Mach number investigation. At 200mph I put the nose down sharply and hit Mach .975, pulling out at

around 3,000 feet above the lake bed. As we were somewhat short on power, the XF10F-1 had to be taken high and dived steeply, but I never reached the critical Mach number or encountered compressibility effects. The accompanying F-86 Sabre chase plane was going flat out in the dive but was soon trailing behind.

On the 23rd flight, nine days later, I was flying polars at around 400 mph when my canopy blew up, the plexiglass shattering and leaving only the frame! Buffeted around the cockpit, I hurriedly chopped the engine and the next thing that I remember was the buffeting easing at around 200mph

Reinforced fiberglass canopy which replaced the blown canopy after the 23rd flight. (Grumman)

and gingerly advancing the power to get back to the field. The chase pilot, my old friend Zeke Hopkins, thought that I was a dead duck since all he could see was me rolling around in the cockpit and was unable to rouse me

The forward fuselage of the Jaguar being unloaded from an Air Force C-124 at Edwards AFB. The aircraft was shipped in four pieces: forward fuselage with engine installed, the tail, the crated double-delta tailplane, and the crated wings. (Grumman via Nicolaou)

Above, XF10F-1 on the ramp at Edwards AFB after being assembled. The outer slats are dropped and the flaps are lowered. All leading edges, intake lips and nose probe were natural metal. (Grumman via Nicolaou)

At right, XF10F-1 in flight with T-33 chase plane. (Grumman)

Below, XF10F-1 just prior to touchdown at Muroc Dry Lake and bottom, at point of touchdown. Wheel well areas were light grey and natural metal and the gear struts were blue except for the swivel mechanism above the main gear which was natural metal. (Grumman via Nicolaou)

16

over the radio. In fact, the microphone had become unplugged and I reconnected and let him know that I was alright as soon as the buffeting eased up.

I knew from my extensive taxiing experience with the XF10F-1 that the horizontal tail got into deep trouble if the canopy was open as the airplane slowed down. Even at 120 mph it was uncontrollable, so I knew that I had to put the airplane down very fast ---- around 200 mph. Just before landing, Zeke called me to say that the ejection seat face curtain was fully extended and flapping on the back of the fiberglass section of the canopy frame, a fact confirmed by a glance in the rear-view mirror attached to the front windshield bow. I reached back, grabbed the rubber handle on the curtain and put it between my teeth, thinking to myself, "What a Grade B movie this is!" As the face curtain had gone to full extension, I knew that the seat was "hot" but realized that there was a microswitch on the canopy frame that I presumed would prevent ejection until the frame had been jettisoned. I wasn't all that sure, however, that the microswitch would be effective with the canopy glass gone so, after touching down and slowing to around 100 mph, I hurredly unbuck-

XF10F-1

Projected Characteristics of the Grumman F10F-1 Jaguar as at 1 May 1951 (ie, one year prior to first flight)

Dimensions: Span (minimum sweep), 50 ft 7 in (15.42 m), (maximum sweep), 36 ft 8 in (11.17 m); length, 54 ft 5 in (16.59 m); height, 16 ft 3 in (4.95 m); wing area (minimum sweep), 467 sq ft (43.38 m²), (maximum sweep), 450 sq ft (41.81 m²); minimum sweep angle, 13.5 deg; maximum sweep angle, 42.5 deg.

Weights: Empty, 20,426 lb (9 265 kg); basic, 21,035 lb (9 541 kg); design normal loaded, 27,351 lb (12 406 kg); combat, 27,451 lb (12 452 kg); max take-off, 35,450 lb (16 080 kg); max landing, 27,700 lb (12 564 kg).

Armament: Four 20-mm Mk 12-0 cannon in forward fuselage with 680 rounds plus 48 2·75-in (70-mm) FFAR or 12 5-in (12.7-cm) HPAG beneath wings. Max bomb capacity, 4,000 lb (1 814 kg).

Power Plant: One Westinghouse J40-WE-8 14-stage axial-flow turbojet with normal max thrust of 6,700 lb (3 039 kg), military thrust of 7,400 lb (3 357 kg) and afterburning thrust of 10,900 lb (4 944 kg).

Performance: (At take-off weight of 31,255 lb/14 176 kg) Max speed (normal max thrust), 581 mph (935 km/h) at 5,000 ft (1 524 m); initial climb, 2,900 ft min (14.73 m/sec); time to 20,000 ft (6 096 m), 9·8 min, to 30,000 ft (9 144 m), 20·4 min; service ceiling, 36,500 ft (11 125 m); combat range, 1,670 mls (2 687 km) at 478 mph (769 km/h); take-off distance (no wind), 1,630 ft (497 m), with 25-knot wind, 960 ft (293 m); stalling speed, 112 mph (180 km/h). (At gross weight of 27,451 lb/12 452 kg and with full afterburning) Max speed, 710 mph (1 143 km/h) at sea level; combat speed, 632 mph (1 017 km/h) at 35,000 ft (10 668 m); initial climb, 13,350 ft min (67·82 m/sec); ceiling (500 ft min 2·54 m sec climb rate), 45,800 ft (13 960 m).

PILOT PRESS
COPYRIGHT
DRAWING

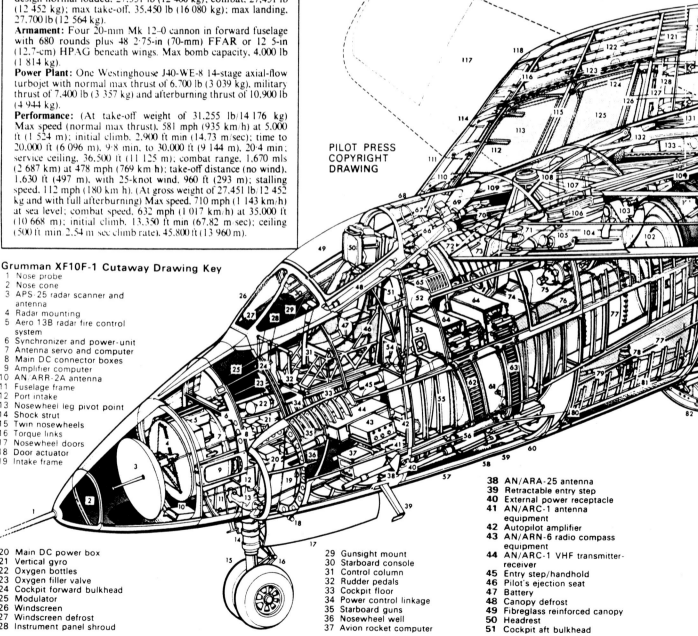

Gruman XF10F-1 Cutaway Drawing Key
1 Nose probe
2 Nose cone
3 APS-25 radar scanner and antenna
4 Radar mounting
5 Aero 13B radar fire control system
6 Synchronizer and power-unit
7 Antenna servo and computer
8 Main DC connector boxes
9 Amplifier computer
10 AN/ARR-2A antenna
11 Fuselage frame
12 Port intake
13 Nosewheel leg pivot point
14 Shock strut
15 Twin nosewheels
16 Torque links
17 Nosewheel doors
18 Door actuator
19 Intake frame

20 Main DC power box
21 Vertical gyro
22 Oxygen bottles
23 Oxygen filler valve
24 Cockpit forward bulkhead
25 Modulator
26 Windscreen
27 Windscreen defrost
28 Instrument panel shroud

29 Gunsight mount
30 Starboard console
31 Control column
32 Rudder pedals
33 Cockpit floor
34 Power control linkage
35 Starboard guns
36 Nosewheel well
37 Avion rocket computer

38 AN/ARA-25 antenna
39 Retractable entry step
40 External power receptacle
41 AN/ARC-1 antenna equipment
42 Autopilot amplifier
43 AN/ARN-6 radio compass equipment
44 AN/ARC-1 VHF transmitter-receiver
45 Entry step/handhold
46 Pilot's ejection seat
47 Battery
48 Canopy defrost
49 Fibreglass reinforced canopy
50 Headrest
51 Cockpit aft bulkhead

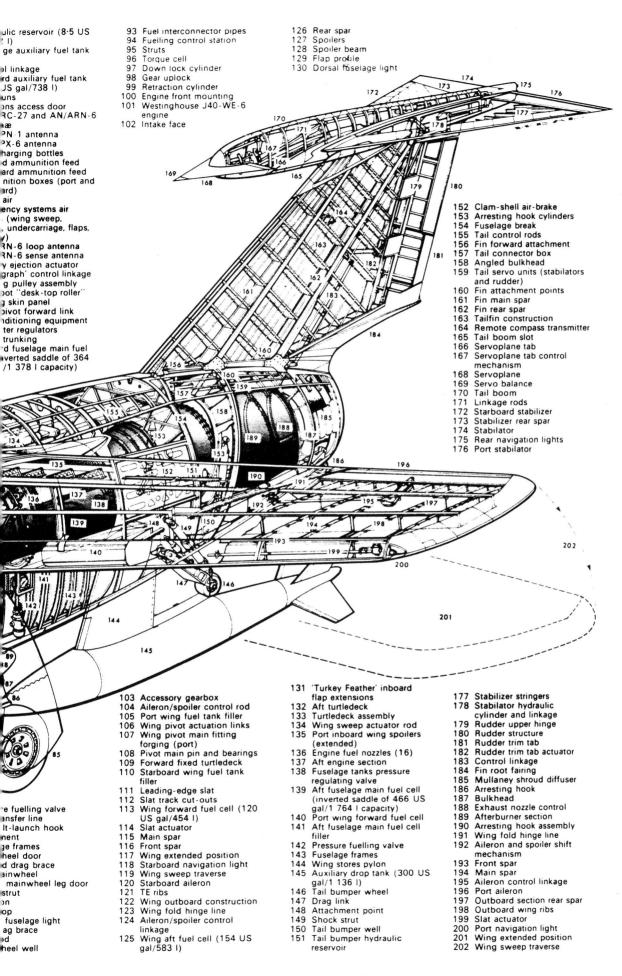

ulic reservoir (8·5 US
 l)
ge auxiliary fuel tank

l linkage
rd auxiliary fuel tank
US gal/738 l)
uns
ns access door
RC-27 and AN/ARN-6
æ
N-1 antenna
X-6 antenna
harging bottles
d ammunition feed
ard ammunition feed
nition boxes (port and
ard)
air
ency systems air
 (wing sweep,
, undercarriage, flaps,
)
N-6 loop antenna
N-6 sense antenna
y ejection actuator
graph' control linkage
g pulley assembly
ot "desk-top roller"
g skin panel
ivot forward link
nditioning equipment
ter regulators
trunking
rd fuselage main fuel
verted saddle of 364
/1 378 l capacity)

93 Fuel interconnector pipes
94 Fuelling control station
95 Struts
96 Torque cell
97 Down lock cylinder
98 Gear uplock
99 Retraction cylinder
100 Engine front mounting
101 Westinghouse J40-WE-6
    engine
102 Intake face

126 Rear spar
127 Spoilers
128 Spoiler beam
129 Flap profile
130 Dorsal fuselage light

152 Clam-shell air-brake
153 Arresting hook cylinders
154 Fuselage break
155 Tail control rods
156 Fin forward attachment
157 Tail connector box
158 Angled bulkhead
159 Tail servo units (stabilators
    and rudder)
160 Fin attachment points
161 Fin main spar
162 Fin rear spar
163 Tailfin construction
164 Remote compass transmitter
165 Tail boom slot
166 Servoplane tab
167 Servoplane tab control
    mechanism
168 Servoplane
169 Servo balance
170 Tail boom
171 Linkage rods
172 Starboard stabilizer
173 Stabilizer rear spar
174 Stabilator
175 Rear navigation lights
176 Port stabilator

103 Accessory gearbox
104 Aileron/spoiler control rod
105 Port wing fuel tank filler
106 Wing pivot actuation links
107 Wing pivot main fitting
    forging (port)
108 Pivot main pin and bearings
109 Forward fixed turtledeck
110 Starboard wing fuel tank
    filler
111 Leading-edge slat
112 Slat track cut-outs
113 Wing forward fuel cell (120
    US gal/454 l)
114 Slat actuator
115 Main spar
116 Front spar
117 Wing extended position
118 Starboard navigation light
119 Wing sweep traverse
120 Starboard aileron
121 TE ribs
122 Wing outboard construction
123 Wing fold hinge line
124 Aileron/spoiler control
    linkage
125 Wing aft fuel cell (154 US
    gal/583 l)

131 'Turkey Feather' inboard
    flap extensions
132 Aft turtledeck
133 Turtledeck assembly
134 Wing sweep actuator rod
135 Port inboard wing spoilers
    (extended)
136 Engine fuel nozzles (16)
137 Aft engine section
138 Fuselage tanks pressure
    regulating valve
139 Aft fuselage main fuel cell
    (inverted saddle of 466 US
    gal/1 764 l capacity)
140 Port wing forward fuel cell
141 Aft fuselage main fuel cell
    filler
142 Pressure fuelling valve
143 Fuselage frames
144 Wing stores pylon
145 Auxiliary drop tank (300 US
    gal/1 136 l)
146 Tail bumper wheel
147 Drag link
148 Attachment point
149 Shock strut
150 Tail bumper well
151 Tail bumper hydraulic
    reservoir

e fuelling valve
ansfer line
lt-launch hook
nent
ge frames
heel door
d drag brace
ainwheel
 mainwheel leg door
strut
on
op
fuselage light
ag brace
d
heel well

177 Stabilizer stringers
178 Stabilator hydraulic
    cylinder and linkage
179 Rudder upper hinge
180 Rudder structure
181 Rudder trim tab
182 Rudder trim tab actuator
183 Control linkage
184 Fin root fairing
185 Mullaney shroud diffuser
186 Arresting hook
187 Bulkhead
188 Exhaust nozzle control
189 Afterburner section
190 Arresting hook assembly
191 Wing fold hinge line
192 Aileron and spoiler shift
    mechanism
193 Front spar
194 Main spar
195 Aileron control linkage
196 Port aileron
197 Outboard section rear spar
198 Outboard wing ribs
199 Slat actuator
200 Port navigation light
201 Wing extended position
202 Wing sweep traverse

18

led, scrambled out of the cockpit and straddled the front fuselage ahead of the windshield, facing aft. I had managed to get back on the ground and I had no taste for taking-off again in an unattached ejection seat! The XF10F-1 eventually came to a standstill by itself after completing a wide ground loop.

We found out later that the safety pin in the seat, which would have been pulled free by a wire attached to the canopy frame, was barely in its hole and was being held in only by friction. Debris from the canopy must have impinged on the unguarded wire causing the pin to snap over its detent. Why it did not go all the way I shall never know, but my relief at getting out of that seat was more than justified. The port leading-edge wing slats were scored and scratched all

the way to the wingtip, and we concluded that the sliding canopy bow, which was not attached to the rest of the canopy frame, had slid along the wing leading edge when the canopy blew up, the canopy having presumably failed somehow at the bow, cracking from there and blowing out.

The XF10F-1 embodied so many new features that, in retrospect, it seems that the airplane was almost predestined not to succeed. However, the most innovative of these, the variable-sweep wing, was the least of our problems, and I used this feature on every flight without difficulty. Only once did I have a problem related to wing sweeping. On this occasion, the "desk top rollers", which unwound to cover the opening in the fuselage ahead of the leading edge as the wing moved back, creaked, groaned and

"Corky" taxis the Jaguar back across the lake bed after an early flight. Speed brakes have not been added yet. (Grumman via Nicolaou)

ground very slowly as they wound up. Something was obviously wrong, but because it was so protracted. I stopped sweeping the wing and reversed the process. The forward movement of the wings slowed progressively and they did not reach the fully forward position for almost a full minute. Normally the process took between five and ten seconds.

The XF10F-1 on the ramp at Edwards AFB with the rudder fully deflected, flaps down, and the port wing paddle spoilers extended. Note the positioning of the landing gear and their doors. (Grumman via Nicolaou)

On the ground we soon discovered the cause. The hydraulic fluid had been 86 F over its upper temperature limit and had jellied, and I had been trying to push jelly through the pistons. Every hydraulic line had to be taken out, flushed and cleaned, and higher-temperature fluid had to be used. The aerodynamics of the wing were such that it was supposed to unsweep of its own accord if the hydraulics were ever lost. I had believed this feasible until this particular flight but I was subsequently convinced that the wing could never have unswept aerodynamically. It needed some hydraulic assistance because of the trapped hydraulic loads, friction loads, etc.

Incidentally, Gordon Israel and I agreed that the wing sweep handle should act like a throttle (ie, moved forward the airplane would go faster and moved aft the airplane would slow down). The handle was positioned right next to the throttle and used that way --- I thought it was great. Years later, when we got to the F-111 and I suggested a similar arrangement, nobody agreed with me. The handle, it was said, should logically be pulled back to sweep the wings and pushed forward to unsweep them, and that is how it has been ever since. Personally, I still believe this arrangement to be wrong and they still humor me about it.

The Westinghouse J40 was an interesting enough power plant, being very heavy and operating at appreciably lower temperatures than those of its contemporaries. It had big bearings and castings and looked like the turbine for an electric locomotive or a hydroelectric station. If the J40 can be taken as a guideline, Westinghouse was hardly aviation oriented. Because afterburner development was so far behind schedule, the XF10F-1 was never to fly with this power boost, and without afterburner, the J40 could deliver only some 68 percent of the 10,000 pounds of advertised thrust. Consequently, owing to the poor thrust-to-weight ratio of this engine compounded by the airframe

The XF10F-1 accelerates across the lake-bed for a takeoff run. (Grumman)

Even though the aircraft was never operated with the afterburner, the J40 engine is seen here at Edwards AFB fitted with the afterburner extension and insulating blanket. (Grumman via Nicolaou)

weight, the XF10F-1 demanded a takeoff run of over two miles and then reached only 130 mph!

After starting up the J40, one knew when the engine had warmed up because the airplane stopped vibrating, smoothing out after a couple of minutes running. Every once in a while, my chase pilot would announce that a big puff of black smoke had been emitted from my tail. On the first occasions that this happened, I anxiously enquired if he could see any fire, but after getting a negative response several times, I realized that this was simply the way the J40 worked. From time-to-time it would coke up and then expel a big blast of black smoke --- all very unsettling but apparently not dangerous. One thing about the J40 that was more disturbing, however, was the extremely protracted acceleration time. The engine would accelerate to 100 percent rpm and, with further throttle movement, the clamshell would then close and start giving noticeable thrust, but before this happened 100 percent rpm corresponded to only 30 percent military (ie, max non-afterburning) thrust. The engine had a 21-second acceleration time. If it was cut back to idling it took 21 seconds to get the engine up to speed once more and have the clamshell closed, and that can be an awfully long time under some circumstances.

During one landing, I had the engine back to idling and slowed down too much, getting some T-tail pitch-up. I poured on the coals, but the thrust did not pick up until I was about 100 feet above the ground, slowing my descent rate somewhat but, nevertheless, the XF10F-1 hit the lake

bed at more than 20 feet per second. Bob Mullaney said afterwards that he thought that I would hit hard enough for the airplane to disintegrate. I rolled barely 900 feet without braking, and the Secretary of the Navy, for whom we were putting on a show, was convinced that the XF10F-1 was the most phenomenal airplane that he had ever seen. This was, in fact, the ninth flight of the XF10F-1 which took place on 23 June 1952, and the next day, my boss, Bob Hall, called me up and said, "I don't know what kind of an airshow you put on, but the Secretary thought it was great and he's ordered 30 more airplanes!"

One propulsion fix that we undertook on the J40 was to add a Mullaney diffuser to the tailpipe prior to the eleventh flight. With the original engine installation, the XF10F-1 could get up to speeds only of the order of Mach .6 to .7 with the wings unswept and not much better with them swept. It was hard to keep flying in the latter configuration because the aircraft slowed down simply as a result of the high angle of attack. The performance was much lower than had been predicted and Bob Mullaney felt that we should move the tailpipe minimum area aft and reduce the boat tail angle of the XF10F-1's contours, and introduce a somewhat blunter aft end for the engine flow to work on. This change improved the airplane so much that I managed to hit Mach .86 in level flight. The modification greatly reduced the base drag, both engine and airframe, and the cooling drag as well. Prior to this we had even had airflow going forward in the engine cooling shroud.

In addition to sporting the first engine electronic fuel control system, the

XF10F-1 also had the first electronic fuel balancing system. Nevertheless, the tanks would never drain simultaneously; first one tank would empty and then the next. We never did master that fuel balancing system. I flew every test well within the vicinity of Edwards as I never knew if the engine would flameout when a tank emptied. In all the time that I flew the XF10F-1 I never lost the feeling that the fuel system had a mind of its own.

The lateral control system comprised, essentially, eight paddle spoilers per wing. During the demonstration for the Secretary of the Navy in June 1952, I had inadvertently flown 50 knots faster than I had ever gone before with the wings swept. The lateral control had begun to flutter, wrenching the stick from my hands. The stick thrashed back and forth against my legs (I discovered later that I was bruised black and blue) before I could get a hold on it. As the airplane slowed the fluttering ceased. When we measured the hinge moments of the paddle spoilers, these supposedly being zero because they rotated in a plane normal to the wing, we discovered that they were unbelievably erratic.

We tried many different shapes and edges, but nothing was successful, so I flew most subsequent tests with the paddle spoilers blocked out. The small ailerons, which were only meant to provide the system with a certain amount of "feel", had then to be used for roll control, giving a mere 10 degrees per second roll rate!

Control cables actuated the lateral system and with that variable-sweep wing the system suffered tremendous stretch. With someone sitting in the cockpit and holding the stick, I could pull the paddle spoilers out to full deflection. The system incorporated a

21

large parallelogram mechanism --- a pantograph that was supposed to maintain cable tension at any wing and spoiler position --- but this was anything but satisfactory.

The two-segment, full-span, leading-edge slats were automatic, being aerodynamically actuated. They were erratic and never functioned simultaneously. At high "G" and high speed, one of the slats came out on one occasion and very nearly parted company with the rest of the airplane. All of the tracks were broken. Three slats were out and locked

with the fourth jammed and cocked way over to one side! After that I double-checked that the slats were locked up before I did any high-speed flying. At low speeds the airplane was much too unstable with all the slats out, so I made low-speed tests later with the inboard slats locked in the retracted position.

Probably the greatest single source of trouble with the XF10F-1 was the aerodynamically-balanced horizontal tail. The idea was that a conventional stabilizer with trailing-edge elevator would shock out and be

Full scale test rig of the XF10F-1's double-delta "T" tail which gave the program so much trouble. The tail was mounted on a rocket sled which ran on rails to give enough speed to adequately test the design and its modifications. This testing went on independent of the flight test program and was always months behind. (Grumman via Nicolaou)

useless at transonic Mach numbers. It seemed that positioning the elevator in front of the tailplane might avoid the problem. We were conservative and tried to avoid using power-boosted controls, but the main difficulty was that the horizontal tail weighed 1,200 pounds and had a natural frequency of 1.7 seconds, which made it slow to respond. The stick was like rubber; the stick moved and a finite time later the tail moved. The stick activated the little canard servo plane on the horizontal tail boom, the light aerodynamic forces on this small area then eventually moving the entire horizontal tail. After applying progressively more stick input, the tail would finally respond madly and then it had to be corrected in the opposite direction.

On the 17th flight horizontal ventral fins ("horsals") were installed (see page 9 for configuration before the tailcone area was modified). At left, the horsal is seen with a fattened tailcone and a fence added to the base of the vertical fin. (Grumman via Nicolaou)

Various fixes were tried. We fitted counter-balanced springs; we changed the sizes, areas and ratios of the stabilator and servo plane, and we put tabs on the servo plane. I even tried running a set of springs to the seat and to the instrument panel from the stick so that my hand would have something to work against, giving me a better idea where the stick was in relation to tail movement. Nothing really did the trick, however, and I was never to achieve positive control, the tail always doing its own thing and leaving me wondering how I could catch up with it. In the end, we admitted defeat and went to an F9F-6 type powered tail. Had we opted from the outset for a low-set powered tail as on the original mock-up we would have saved ourselves a great deal of woe.

For the 24th flight, on 9 January 1953, we fitted a larger balanced tail to little effect, and this was removed and the smaller tail reinstated for the 27th flight which took place some three months later, on 5 March. On one of the three flight tests that I made with the larger tail fitted, I found myself completely out of phase with the tail at low speed, the airplane bucking uncontrollably around the sky. I should have bailed out but couldn't get out of the cockpit. I shall never know how I regained control on

that flight, having not the slightest idea what I or the airplane did to recover. Of one thing I was sure: the balanced tail was never going to function satisfactorily. The canard had too much inertia and too little aspect ratio for the control power required at low speeds. The faster the XF10F-1 went the better the tail felt and in high speed dives I had 50 pounds of stick force per "G". Indeed, it was so stable that I could not move it! Yet at low speeds it was so unstable as to be virtually uncontrollable. I have since told myself that if I had been older or smarter I would have quit sooner.

When we finally got around to fitting a powered conventional F9F-6 tail, the XF10F-1 was great, but this change was not made until the 29th flight on 23 April 1953, and by that time nearly a year of flight testing had elapsed and the remaining days in the active life of Grumman's highly novel prototype were strictly numbered.

Not only did we have difficulties with the horizontal tail --- the vertical tail also offered its share of problems. When I pushed full rudder, there was so much stretch in the cables that I got only some five degrees of movement rather than 30 degrees! There was also strong fin and boat tail buffeting. At that time, vortex generators were supposed to cure any buffet problem.

If you could think of no other way to cure buffeting you slapped on some vortex generators. Unfortunately, the XF10F-1 was apparently oblivious of this "fact"; vortex generators were eventually applied to the fin and around the tailpipe without the slightest effect.

From a test pilot's point of view, the flight test program conducted with the variable-sweep Grumman was unbelievably interesting. We were continuously improvising; always changing things. As Bob Mullaney once put it, "every flight was a first flight!" I had never attended a test pilot's school, but for me, the XF10F-1 provided the complete curriculum. If it taught us anything, we learned the hard way that we should never put so many innovative items in one airplane. For a year we tried to break all the rules of aerodynamics, but the protracted development difficulties that were experienced, added to the availability of the more conventional Cougar, finally led Grumman to admit defeat and abandon this little-known "cat".

New turtledeck installation fitted to the Jaguar for testing on flights 27 and 28. When the wing was in the unswept position the venitian blind style wing fillets would roll closed. (Grumman)

The Jaguar as configured for the last three flights with the F9F-6 tail installed instead of the double-delta tail. The center photo shows the tail bumper extended and the perforations for the speed brakes can be seen through the national insignia. (MFR)

XF10F-1 JAGUAR FLIGHT TEST SUMMARY

NO	DATE	DURATION	REMARKS
01	05-19-52	16 MIN.	Excessive trim change with flaps; rudder buffet and yaw at high power.
02	05-21-52	30 MIN.	Explosion in engine; dead stick landing; trim with flaps corrected.
03	05-22-52		General evaluation.
04	05-23-52	35 MIN.	Two loud explosions; fire warning light at full throttle due to flow on detection line.
05	06-03-52	40 MIN.	Low speed characteristics; stalls; tufts on fin.
06	06-03-52	45 MIN.	Longitudinal flight characteristics; spoiler flutter.
07	06-10-52	22 MIN.	General characteristics; arresting hook slot sealed with fabric; conical spoiler edges.
08	06-11-52	45 MIN.	Lateral over-control; slat cut only upon rough part of runway during landing.
09	06-23-52	21 MIN.	Demonstration for Secretary of the Navy.
10	06-26-52	32 MIN.	Lateral directional characteristics.
11	07-14-52	24 MIN.	Mullaney diffuser installed.
12	07-17-52	49 MIN.	Nosewheel lift-off; takeoff runs; various slat combinations.
13	07-18-52	25 MIN.	Forward CG; lateral check.
14	07-21-52		Directional characteristics.
15	07-21-52	40 MIN.	Lateral check to Mach .8.
16	07-22-52	51 MIN.	Lateral longitudinal check with slats in operation; overtemped hydraulic fluid.
17	09-09-52	42 MIN.	Horizontal ventral fins; flap ends cut out; spoilers sealed; wing stop at any angle; speed brakes.
18	09-12-52	32 MIN.	Speed brake vibration.
19	10-10-52	38 MIN.	Very poor performance due to engine fuel adjustment error; flight abandoned.
20	10-11-52	43 MIN.	High Mach dives.
21	10-13-52	46 MIN.	Low speed airspeed calibration with T-28 aircraft.
22	10-14-52	42 MIN.	Medium speed airspeed calibration with F-86.
23	10-20-52	32 MIN.	Canopy blown off; right side of aircraft tufted.
24	01-09-53	54 MIN.	Larger balanced tail; new fuselage aft end; spoilers unsealed for this flight.
25	01-10-53	41 MIN.	Performance check.
26	01-13-53	41 MIN.	Spoilers sealed; cutouts on flap ends closed.
27	03-05-53	30 MIN.	Smaller tail re-installed; new turtle deck; turkey feathers on flaps; spoilers unsealed.
28	03-06-53	62 MIN.	Very poor lateral control with wings swept; Vortex generators off aft end.
29	04-23-53	15 MIN.	F9F-6 powered tail; horsa's removed; lateral power boost; heavy nosedown trim terminated flight.
30	04-24-53	52 MIN.	Very good lift for control surface size; again poor slat operation.
31	04-24-53	54 MIN.	Slats locked up; improved speed versus power; still lateral problems.
32	04-25-53	67 MIN.	Speed brake buffeting; poor directionally without horsal fins; little trim change with wing sweep.

INSTRUMENT PANEL MOCK-UP OF XF10F-1 JAGUAR

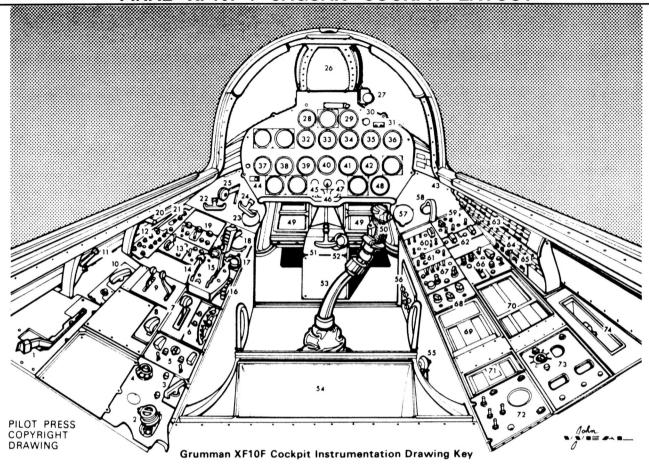

PILOT PRESS
COPYRIGHT
DRAWING

Grumman XF10F Cockpit Instrumentation Drawing Key

1 Emergency control: wing sweep and slat lock release
2 Composite disconnect (oxygen, radio, anti-G suit)
3 Emergency brake handle
4 Pilot's anti-G suit control
5 Trim tab control panel:
   Rudder tab control selector switch (nose left, nose right)
   Emergency power switch (aileron tab)
   Emergency power switch (rudder tab)
   Emergency aileron tab control switch (left wing down, right wing down)
   Emergency rudder tab control switch (nose left, nose right)
6 Servo plane trim tab control
7 Wing flaps control
8 Slat latch control
9 Boom and servoplane dampers control panel:
   Boom damper control lever
   Servoplane damper control lever
   Slat latch control switch (OFF — unlock)
10 Emergency flap control
11 Pre-ejection lever
12 AC fuse panel:
   G-2 compass fuses A and B
   Fast erecting Gyro fuses A and B
   Fuel gauge fuse
   Three (3) spares
13 Fuel control panel:
   Selector switch (wing tanks, drop tanks)
   Wing tanks purge switch (purge — normal)
   Fuselage auxiliary tank switch (ON — OFF)
   Fuselage auxiliary tank empty light
   Wing tank empty light (left, right)
14 Wing sweep control handle
15 Throttle control lever
16 Throttle and wing sweep levers friction control

17 Trim tab position indicators
18 Oxygen regulator
19 Engine control panel:
   Anti-icing switch
   Anti-icing ON indicator light
   Press to start engine button switch
   Emergency pump press button switch
   Primary pump failed indicator light
   Emergency regulator ON indicator light
   Fuel regulator switch (select emergency — reset)
20 Canopy control
21 Pylon jettison panel:
   Pylon jettison arming switch (OFF — ON)
   Press to jettison pylon button switch
22 Canopy jettison handle
23 Wheels and flaps position indicator
24 Emergency landing gear handle
25 Landing gear control handle
26 Windscreen
27 Standby compass
28 Altimeter
29 Max allowable air speed indicator
30 Wing slat lock indicator
31 Fire warning light
32 Tailpipe temperature indicator
33 Tachometer
34 Gyro horizon indicator
35 Accelerometer
36 ADF indicator
37 Fuel gauge wing tanks
38 Fuel gauge fuselage auxiliary tank
39 Fuel gauge forward fuselage main fuel cell
40 Fuel gauge aft fuselage main fuel cell
41 Turn and bank indicator
42 Directional Gyro compass indicator
43 Canopy frame
44 Fuel gauge test button

45 Clock
46 Oil pressure gauge
47 Oil temperature gauge
48 Fuel flowmeter
49 Rudder pedals
50 Control grip (communications/weapons buttons)
51 Rudder pedal adjustment handle
52 Relief tube
53 Control column
54 Pilot's seat
55 Seat height control lever
56 Precision meters pin jacks
57 Cabin altimeter
58 Arresting hook control
59 Air conditioning control panel:
   Cabin air conditioning selector (Hot — cold — defrost)
   Cabin air conditioning switch (Auto — OFF — standby)
   Standby temperature switch (Hot — cold)
   Ram air switch (More — less)
60 Test panel
61 Electric auxiliary panel:
   G-2 compass switch (Compass control — free DG)
   Gyro-horizon fast erector light
   Gyro-horizon fast erector switch (Normal — OFF)
   Pitot heater switch (ON — OFF)
62 Electric master switch panel:
   Fuel master switch (ON — OFF)
   Engine master switch (ON — OFF)
63 Circuit breaker panel
64 Light fuses panel:
   Panel lights fuse and spare
   Engine instruments fuse and spare
   Flight instruments fuse and spare

65 Fire extinguisher switches
66 Electric power panel:
   DC power switch (Battery and generator — OFF — battery only)
   Generator warning lights, No 1, No 2 (ON — no output)
   AC power selector switch (AC generator — OFF — external power)
   AC generator field switch (OFF — ON)
   Inverter selector switch (Standby — normal)
   Inverter warning light
67 Exterior lights panel
68 Interior lights panel:
   Flight instrument lights rheostat
   Engine instrument lights rheostat
   Panel lights rheostat
69 AN/ARC-1 control panel
70 AN/ARN-6 radio compass panel
71 Wing fold and lock control panel (Instruments not fitted for first flights)
72 Hydraulic panel:
   Hydraulic pump pressure gauge
   Auxiliary hydraulic pump switch (ON — OFF)
   Pre-combat switch (Combat-normal) for hydraulic system and cabin pressure
   Fuel tank vent switch (Vent — normal)
73 Voltmeter panel:
   Voltmeter selector switch (Variable freq. ØA, ØB, ØC and fixed freq. ØA, ØB, ØC)
   AC voltmeter
   DC voltmeter — No. 1 generator
   DC voltammeter — No. 2 generator
74 Map and chart case

LEFT PILOT'S CONSOLE ON THE XF10F-1 JAGUAR

RIGHT PILOT'S CONSOLE ON THE XF10F-1 JAGUAR

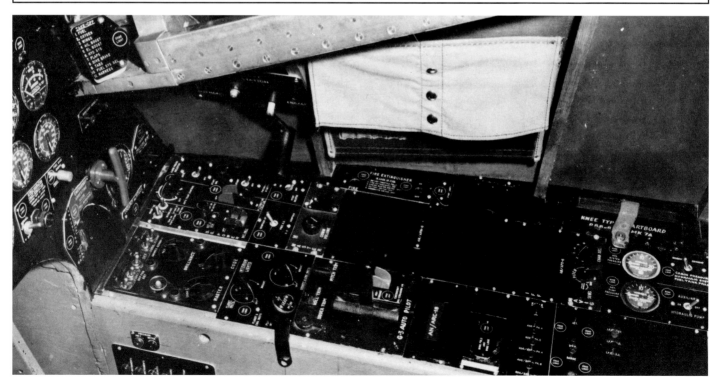

ESOTERIC MODELS 1:72 SCALE VACUFORM XF10F-1 JAGUAR KIT

BY STEVE GINTER

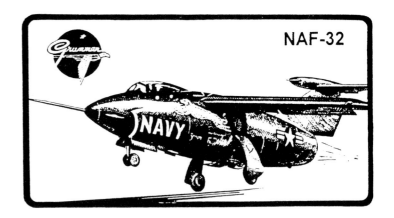

The impetus for this book was the release of the Esoteric kit. I found kit number NAF-32 to be an excellent vacuform kit which went together quickly and easily. The accuracy and shape of the kit compares favorably with photos and drawings. The kit is comprised of two white plastic vacuform sheets, one vacuformed canopy, seventeen white metal pieces, a decal sheet and a very good set of 1:72 scale drawings.

The two white vacuform sheets are made of good quality plastic which has an excellent thickness to scale ratio. The panel lines are accurately placed and not too heavy or light. The clear vacuform canopy has good clarity and was not too brittle to work with.

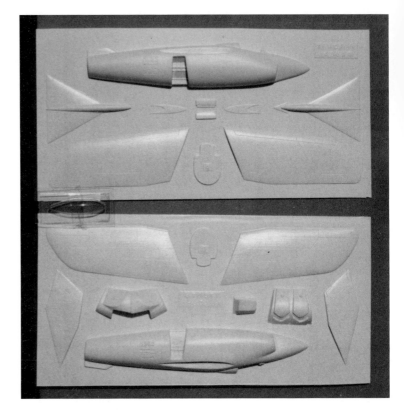

The seventeen white metal pieces are crisp and free of flash. The only discrepancy was that the nose gear scissors were not included on the nose gear or in the kit. The white metal nose test boom is molded with a bent tip, which is correct, so don't straighten it. A small gear door must also be cut from scrap plastic for the tail wheel bumper.

The decal sheet was nicely done and complete except for panel door stencils which look just as real when they are hand-painted. The adhesive material for the decals was too milky and required me to wash off the excess a couple of times. The opaque qualities of the white stars was not up to standards and you may want to replace them with some from the spares box.

The instruction sheet does not give adequate explanations on how to assemble the main gear parts. There are two white metal box-like pieces which I didn't figure out how to use until I had assembled one side. They are used to mount the gear doors to the main gear. You also have to play with positioning the gear to give you the proper fuselage to ground clearance. I miscalculated the clearance on the nose gear and built the kit with the nose gear leg too long.

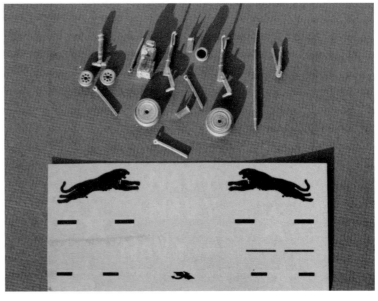

I achieved excellent wing fit with no filling by cutting the lower wing pieces as shown in the instruction sheet and by leaving the upper wing uncut. I then cut out the upper half of the wing roots to accommodate the upper wing halves. I would also recommend that either a fuselage bulkhead be installed near the tailpipe or an exhaust cone from the spares box be utilized for strength.

COMBAT MODELS 1:48 SCALE XF10F-1 JAGUAR

BY STEVE GINTER

The 1:48 scale Combat vacuform kit dates from the early 1980s and is fairly accurate except for the nose profile which is too narrow, pointed and not fat enough. The panel detail is good, but suffers from quite a few mold marks. The kit is straightforward and goes together fairly fast.

The kit is molded on one sheet of white plastic which is a bit too thin for my liking, but of good quality. The vacuformed canopy has excellent clarity, but it's shape where it meets the fuselage does not match. So I went to the spares box and modified a FJ-3 windscreen and cut the rear canopy of a TF-18A to fit. The kit also comes with three white metal landing gear parts, which are well made and work well on the kit. There are no decals, so they must come from the spares box, except that the Jaguar must be hand painted.

When I built the kit I utilized cockpit parts from the spares box as well as a plastic exhaust pipe to add stiffness to the rear of the fuselage. I also had to construct several bulkheads to use as fuselage stiffeners. This was my first experience in constructing a 1:48 scale vacuform kit and I found it much more difficult than vacuform projects built in 1:72 scale.

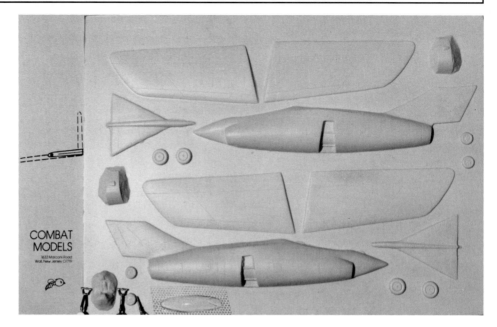

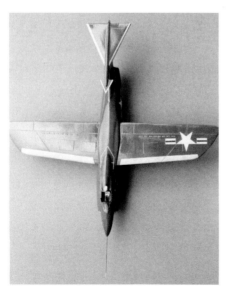

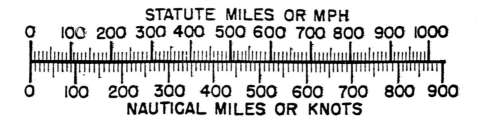

STATUTE MILES OR MPH

NAUTICAL MILES OR KNOTS

PERFORMANCE SUMMARY					
LOADING CONDITION		(1) FIGHTER	(5) FIGHTER 24 x 2.75" Rockets	(6) GROUND ATTACK 2-2,000# Bombs	(7) LONG RANGE FIGHTER 2-300 Gal.Tank
TAKE-OFF WEIGHT	lbs.	31,255	32,565	35,450	35,370
Fuel (Fixed/Drop)	lbs.	9,510/-	9,510/-	9,510/-	9,510/3,600
Bombs	lbs.	---	---	4,000	---
Wing/Power Loading (A)lbs/sq.ft;lbs/bhp.		67.0/-	69.7/-	75.9/-	75.7/-
Stall Speed--Power off	kn.	99.4	101.5	105.9	105.7
Stall Speed--Power off - No Fuel	kn.	82.8	85.4	90.5	83.8
Stall Speed--Power on	kn.	97.0	99.0	103.1	103.1
Maximum Speed/Alt (B)	kn/ft.	506/5,000	490/12,500	488/12,500	482/12,500
Take-off Distance, deck -- calm	ft.	1,630(3,040)	1,800(3,340)	2,200(4,170)	2,190(4,140)
Take-off Distance, deck 25 kn.	ft.	960(1,808)	1,075(1,970)	1,340(2,575)	1,340(2,555)
Take-off Distance, Airport	ft.	---	---	---	---
Rate of climb -- sea level (B)	ft/min.	2,900	2,480	2,200	2,090
Service Ceiling (B)	ft.	36,500	30,700	29,000	27,800
Time-to-climb 20,000 ft. (B)	min.	9.8	12.1	14.1	15.4
Time-to-climb 30,000 ft. (B)	min.	20.4	32.9	---	---
Combat Range/V av (Climb) ft. n.mi/kn.		1,450/415	1,150/407	1,045/411	1,815/413
Combat Radius/V av (F-5) ft. n.mi/kn.		550/415	445/414	---	745/414
Combat Radius/V av (Grd.Attack) n.mi./kn		---	---	300/415	---
LOADING CONDITION		(2) COMBAT	(3) COMBAT	(4) COMBAT	
GROSS WEIGHT	lbs.	27,451	27,451	27,451	
Engine power		Mil. + A.B.	Military	Normal	
Fuel	lbs.	5,706	5,706	5,706	
Bombs/Tanks		---	---	---	
Max. speed at sea level	kn.	617(568)	550(517)	504(494)	
Max. speed/Alt	kn/ft.	617/S.L.	554/5,500	525/7,500	
Combat speed/Alt	kn/ft.	549(501)/35000	498(471)/35000	(463)/35,000	
Rate of climb SL	ft/min.	13,350(12,800)	4,110(4,410)	3,150(3,750)	
Ceiling for 500 fpm R/C	ft.	45,800(48,200)	32,400(38,500)	27,500(36,000)	
Time-to-climb/Alt.	min/ft.	4.5(4.6)/35000	(16.5)/35,000	(20.2)/35,000	

(A) BHP at Maximum Critical Altitude
(B) Normal BHP -

NOTES

The J-40-WE-8 is designed for JP-3 fuel. This chart is calculated on the assumption that gasoline may be used with no performance change at equal weights of fuel.

Performance is based on calculations. Range and radius are based on engine specification fuel consumption data increased by 5%.

Take-off distances are with take-off thrust (afterburning). The take-off distances in parentheses are with military thrust (no afterburning).

Spotting: 200 ft. length is required to spot 10 airplanes on the 96 ft. wide deck immediately aft of the forward ramp on the CV-9 class carriers.

CONFIDENTIAL

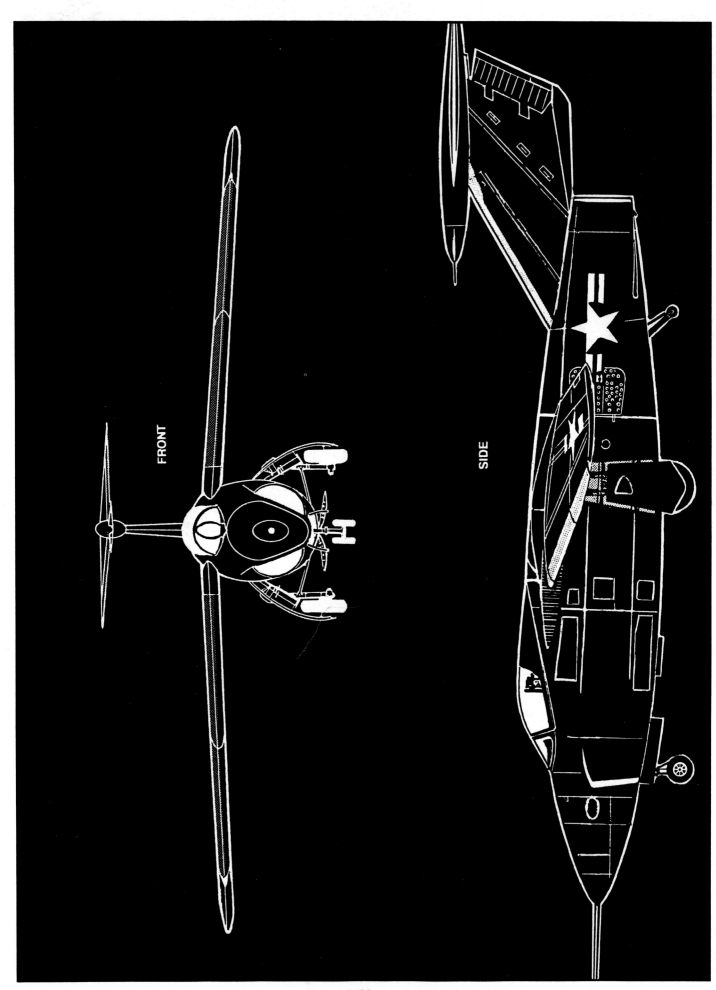

FRONT

SIDE